First Stage
Reader

Thomas A. Velasquez and Ruth Lind Velasquez

*Dedicated to people
entering the world of print where
education, adventure, information
and the future are waiting
to be explored.*

FIRST STAGE READER

Second Revised Edition © 2015
Revised Edition © 2011
Original Copyright © 2000
By Thomas A. and Ruth L. Velasquez
First Stage Publishing Company

Authors: Thomas A. Velasquez and Ruth L. Velasquez
Illustrator: Elia Velasquez Murray
Assistant Editor: Cheramie Leo

First Stage Reader

Books are keys to wisdom's treasure;
Books are gates that lead to pleasure;
Books are paths that upward lead;
Books are friends. Come, let us read.

Emily Paulsson,
American writer, editor, illustrator

1

Alphabet Song

Sing the Alphabet Song with the readers to the tune of Twinkle Twinkle Little Star
By Jane Taylor (September 23, 1783- April 13, 1824)

The Alphabet

Two families live in the Alphabet: the Vowel Family and the Consonant Family. The members of both families are letters. Letters make up words we can say or read.

The Vowel Family is small but very friendly. Vowels are in every English word. The vowels are named **A, E, I, O,** and **U**. Every vowel may represent a long vowel sound or a short vowel sound.

Letters **Y** and **W** are in both families and are called semi-vowels. At the beginning of words, **Y** and **W** belong in the Consonant Family. The Letters **Y** and **W** belong to the Vowel Family when they are with another Vowel in the middle or at the end of a word.

Vowels use their long name sounds in words
☀ when they are by themselves at the end of a one-sound word like *me, my, no* and *go*
☀ when they are beside another vowel as in *pie, maid* or *coat,* and
☀ when the they are standing one consonant letter away from another Vowel as in the words *cake, plate, note* or *time.*

Story

The Long Vowels say, "I use my long vowel sound when another Vowel is only one consonant away. I use my short vowel sound when I am the only Vowel in a word with a Consonant on my right, or when I am in between two Consonants."

"When two Vowels go walking, the vowel on the left makes the sound. The Vowel on the right is quiet." However there are times when **ei** and **ea** do not follow that saying. We will learn more about these vowels in chapters 6 and 13.

Together, the Vowels and Consonants create the words that make up the stories, books, poems, jokes, and songs that help people enjoy and learn when they read.

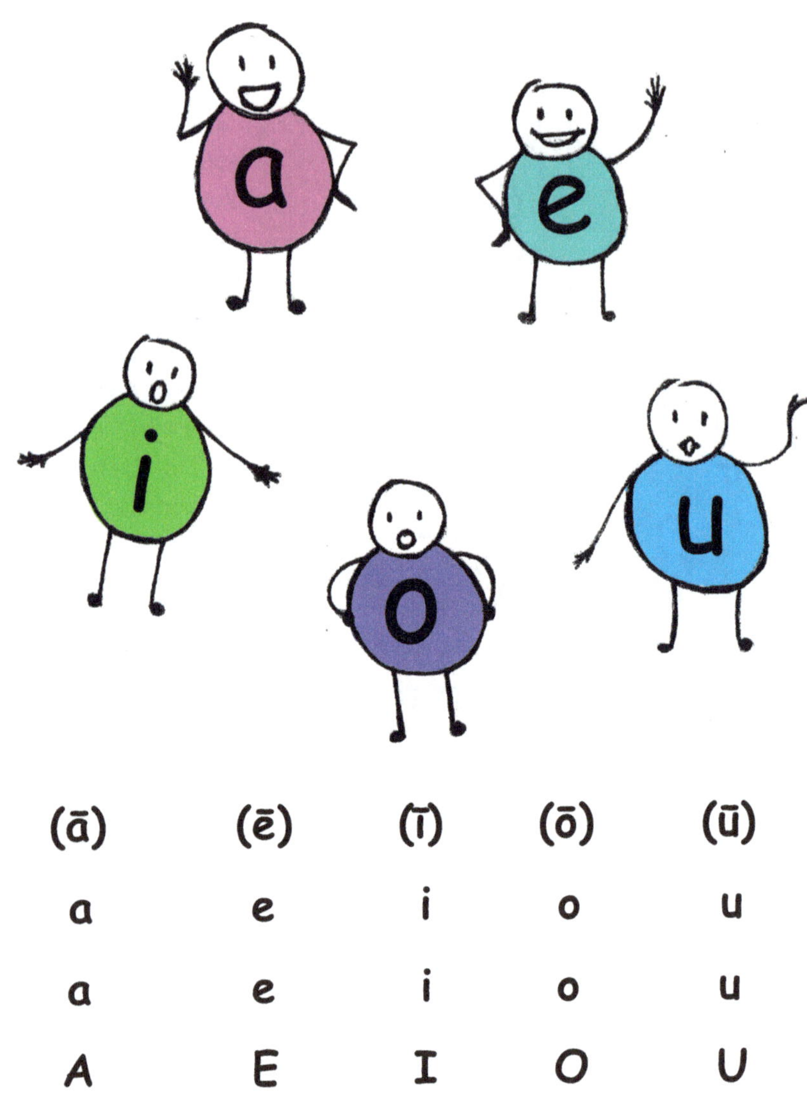

Sing the Long Vowel Song to the tune of BINGO.

ā
a y
ā
e y
ī
u y
ō
o w

B b

Sing the Syllable Song to the tune of BINGO.

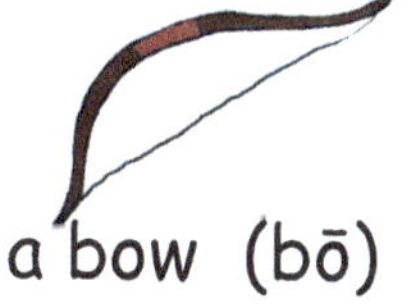

a bow (bō)

a bee (bē)

a bow (bō)

| by (bī) | bye (bī) | buy (bī) |
| be (bē) | Bea (bē) | bay (bā) |

bay	by	bye	bow
buy	bay	bee	by
Bea	bow	buy	be

A Bee by Bea

Bea, a bee by you!
A bee by Bea?
Bye, Bea.
Bye, bye, bee!

S s

say (sā) see (sē) so (sō) Sue (soo)
sees (sēz) sea (sē) buys (bīz)

say see be sea so Sue
sees be bay by bye buys
be bay bee Bea bay buy

Sue

Sue sees Bea.
Sue sees bees by Bea
Bea sees Sue.
I see Bea. I see Sue.
I see bees by Bea.

Sue's Bows

Sue buys bows.
See Sue's bows.
Bea sees Sue's bows.
See Sue's bows?

Bo's Bow

See Bo's bow?
I see Bo's bow.
Sue sees Bo's bow.
Bea sees Bo's bow.
You see Bo's bow.

K k

Kay (kā) Kay's (kāz)

key (kē) keys (kēz)

0 1 2 3 4 5 6 7 8 9

Kay's Keys

I see 3 keys.

Bea sees Kay's 3 keys.

See Kay's 3 keys.

I see Kay's keys.

I see Kay's 3 keys.

Bo's Key

I see Bo's key.

I see Bo's key by Kay's keys.

I see 4 keys.

a	I	you	be	by	so
bee	Bea	bay	say	Kay	you
bays	keys	Bea's	seas	sees	bees
Sue's	bows	bye	bow	key	bay

Kay's Bows

Kay buys Sue's bows. I see Kay buy Sue's bows, so I buy Sue's bows. I buy 2 bows. Kay buys 1 bow.

Bees by Bea

Bo sees bees by Bea.
I see Bea's bees.
I say, "Bye, bye, Bea.
Bye, Bo. Bye, bees."

2

C c (k)

Kay's Cakes
Kay bakes cakes.
I see Kay's cakes.
You see Kay's cakes?
I buy Kay's cakes.

Bo's Bike
I see Bo's bike.
Bo bikes by Sue.
I see Bo bike by Sue.

Kay's Cubes
Kay buys 4 cubes.
I see Kay use 2 cubes.
I say, "Kay, use 4
cubes. I use 4 cubes."

C   c   (s)

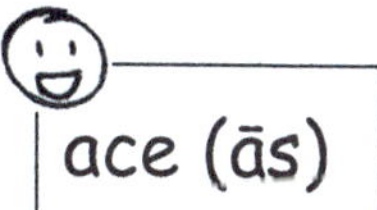

1, 2, 3, 4
I see Bo's ace.
I see Sue's ace.
I see Bea's ace.
I see Kay's ace.
I see 4 aces.

Ice Cubes

Bea uses 3 ice cubes.
Kay sees Bea's ice cubes.
Kay buys 2 ice cubes.
I see 5 ice cubes.

D d

Sue's Dice

Sue buys 2 dice.
Do you see Sue's 2 dice?
I see Sue use 2 dice.

Bo Bikes

Day by day, Bo bikes by a bay. Do you see Bo bike? I see Bo bike. Day by day, I see Bo bike by a bay.

Does

"I see does. Do you see does, Bea?"

"I do. I see 2 does."

"You see 2 does. So do I."

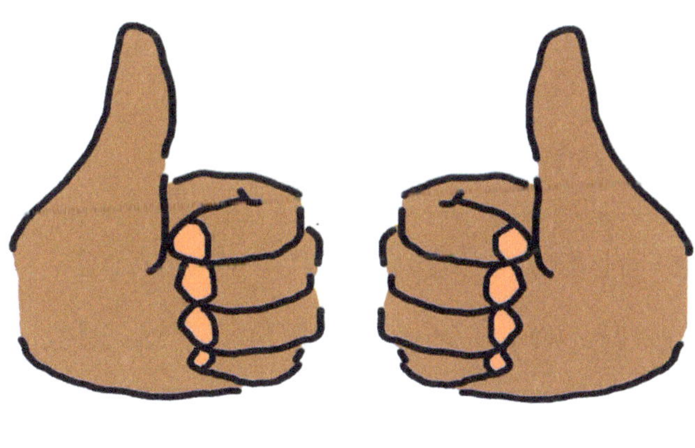

b

bay
be
bye
bow
by
bead

d

day
dye
die
dice
doe
deed

_d _ed

_ed = (t)	_ed = (d)	_ed = (ud)
bake (bāk)	dye (dī)	bead (bēd)
baked (bākt)	dyed (dīd)	beaded (bēd·ud)

ice iced	sue sued	aid aided
cake caked	dye dyed	code coded
base based	bow bowed	seed seeded
dice diced	key keyed	side sided

Seed Cakes

Sue baked seed cakes. Bea aided Sue. Bea iced Sue's cakes.

Abe said, "I buy Sue's iced seed cakes."

T t

tie   it   boat   bat   Kate   cat
bite   bit   coat   cot   tote   tot
seat   set   cute   cut   kite   kit

say (sā)   said (sed)   says (sez)

Abe's tie

Kate's tea set

Abe Said, Kate Said

Abe said "Cute tea set, Kate."

Kate said, "Cute tie, Abe. Did you tie it?"

"I did, Kate. I did tie it."

to (too)   too (too)   two (too)

two = 2

Abe's Cot

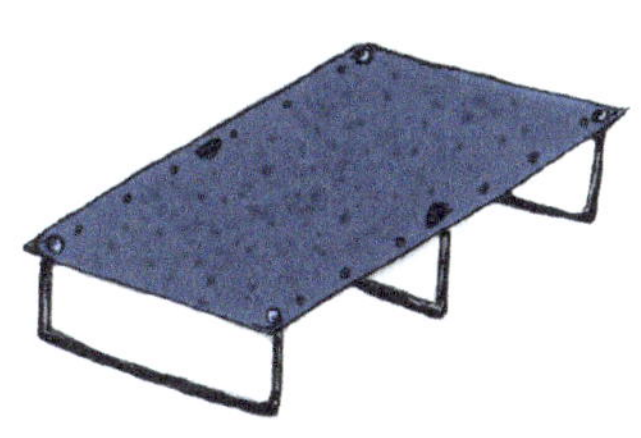

Ed's cat sits by Abe's cot. Abe's coat is by Abe's cot, too. Ed's cat is by Abe's coat. See the cat. See Abe's coat. See the cat by Abe's coat.

Ed's Cat

Ed's cat Ted is a cute cat. Ted totes Ed's coat to Ed.

Abe says, "Too bad Ted bites Ed's coat."

Abe teases Ted. Abe says, "Bad cat."

But Ed says, "Ted is a cute cat."

A Cute Toad

A cute toad sat by Kate as Kate ate two cakes.

"Do you eat cake, Toad?" said Kate.

"I do," said Toad.

Kate said, "You eat cake? Take a cake to eat."

Toad took Kate's cake and ate it.

Ed's Kite

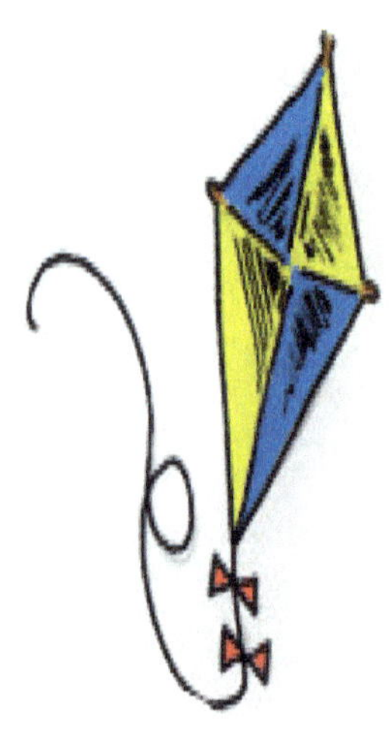

Bea said, "Do you see a kite, Abe?"

"I do," said Abe. "Do you see it?"

"I do!" said Bea.

"Is it Ed's kite?" said Abe.

"It is. It is Ed's kite," said Bea.

M m

am	aim	make	Sam	same
my	sum	mice	man	main
met	meat	meet	dim	dime
mad	maid	made	Tim	time

Tom's Team

Tom's team beat Mike's team. Tom's team beamed.

"Too bad, Mike," said Tom.

Mike said, "I am not sad. Meet you at two. See you."

Mike's team met Tom's team at two.

N n

nine   not   note   need   net   nut
mine   an   man   sent   cone   sink

and   men   tan   den   tone   sand
band   ten   mend   moon   tent   soon

kn = n

know (nō)   knows (nōz)   known (nōn)

knee   knead   knot

Dan's Name

"Do you know my name?" Dan asked Nan.

"No," said Nan. "I do not, and I need it for my notes."

"I do," said Ben. "It is Dan."

"Dan?" asked Nan.

"Yes," said Dan. "Take a note. My name is Dan."

Nine Mice Names

Ken said, "My nine mice need names."

Bea said, "I can name nine names. I know nine nice names: Dan, Kate, Ben, Don, Tom, Tim, Mike, Sue and Nan."

"Nice names, Bea," said Ken.

Notes

Ben sent a note to Ned. Ben's note said, "I need meat by noon."

Ned sent a note to Dan. Ned's note to Dan said, "Ben needs meat by noon. Can you send it?"

Dan sent a note to Ned. Dan's note said, "I can send the meat by noon."

P p

pie

peas in a pod

cap	cape	pin	pine	Pete	pet	paid
tape	tap	pep	peep	pipe	pun	pad

tip	up	cop	cap	keep
sip	cup	top	tap	deep
dip	pup	mop	nap	seep

To Do

Pat a pup.
Take a nap.
Peep at my map.
Put on a cap and cape.
Send a note to Mom.
Be nice to Pete.
Pick a tape.

Time to Eat Cake

Tom said, "Sam, it is 12 p.m., time to eat a cake I baked at 8 a.m. Do you eat cake?"

Sam said, "I do, Tom. Do you take tea at noon?"

"I do," said Tom.

Sam and Tom sat and ate Tom's cake and took tea at 12 p.m.

A Note to Pete

Pete,

Can you keep my pet pup, Pip? Pip is tame and is as neat as a pin. Pip eats meat pies and bones and is a nice pup. I need you to keep Pip.
Pat

Pat,

I can keep Pip for two days. See you soon!
Pete

G g (g) as in go

goat   gob   gum   gap   gas   go
game   gain   got   gale   gate   gut

bug   tug   mug   nag   snug   bog
bag   dog   sag   peg   snag   dug

Pug

My dog Pug goes to my gate. I say "Stop," and Pug stops. Pug does not go past my gate. Pug is a good pup.

Ann's Pig

Ann used my cape. Ann needed my cape to keep snug, but Ann's big pig Pat dug in mud and tugged on my cape. Pat got mud gobs on Ann and on my cape.

_ng

sang   sing   sung   song   bang   gong
king   sting   stung   ding   tongs   ping

Kate and Sue's CD

Kate and Sue sang ten songs.

Tim put Sue and Kate's ten songs on CDs. Tim gave a CD to Tom.

Tom said, "Kate and Sue's CD made my day."

Gongs and Songs

Ann buys gongs. Kate buys gongs too. Ann and Kate bang and ping gongs and sing songs.

"Stop!" says Bea. "No bangs, no songs, no gongs. Stop!"

Ann and Kate stop.

Adding _ing

tape   taping   make   making
tap   tapping   nap   napping
go   going   be   being
mean   meaning   sing   singing

Ann's Song

Ann is good at making songs, and Anne's gang is good at singing. Ann is banging a gong and singing a song. Anne's foot is tapping as Ann is singing. Anne's gang is singing Ann's song, too.

Singing and Tapping

Kate asked Sam, "Do you sing?"

"I do. I do sing," Sam said.

"I sing, too," Kate said.

"Singing is nice. Tapping is nice, too. I tap. Do you tap?"

"I sing and tap, too," said Sam. "Tapping and singing make my day."

4

1 = one

Sing some songs.   I tapped once.

None can go.   Make one bag.

I am done.   Come at once.

Don's Cake

One day Meg came to see Pam.

Meg said, "I need a cake. Don is coming to eat. Can you bake a cake to make Don's day?"

"I can," said Pam.

Meg asked, "Can you bake Don's cake at once?"

Pam said, "I am baking two nice cakes. One can be Don's cake."

_ck

knack   deck   pick   knock   stack

back   neck   kick   dock   duck

tack   peck   sock   stuck   tuck

Pat's Duck

Pat's duck Mick pecked at Matt's seed cakes.

Matt said, "Mick is a pain in my neck. Mick eats my seed cakes. Pat, stick Mick in a sack and take Mick back."

Pat picked up Mick and tucked Mick into a sack.

"Say bye to Matt, Mick," said Pat. Mick's beak stuck up and Mick peeked at Matt.

H h

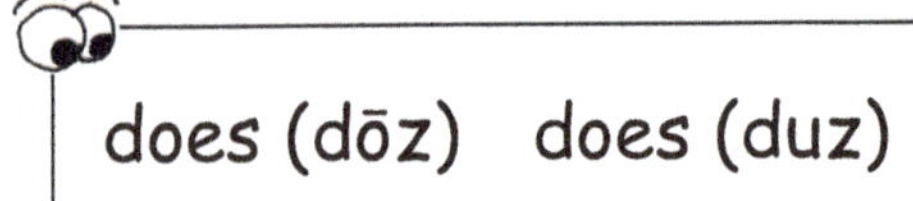

does (dōz)   does (duz)

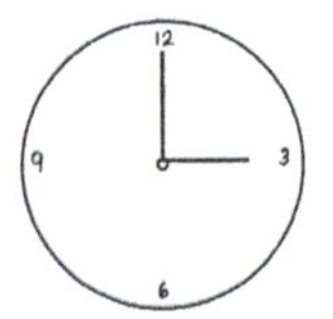

hands 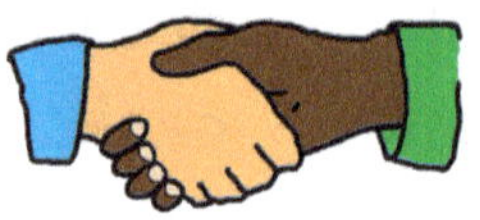

hit	he	hay	hose	heat	his
hike	home	him	hen	had	ham
hunt	hop	hope	hid	hide	hum

Hank's Hike

Hank put on his hat to go hiking and to see some does by a pond. Hank asked Ned to go hiking, too.

Ned said, "It is too hot to hike, Hank. I am going home."

Don's Hen

I cannot find Don's hen. Don says his hen hides in a haystack to make a home. Heat can make a hen hide deep in hay. I hope Don's hen does not get too hot.

_th_

the (thuh)	the (thē)	they (thā)
thick (thik)	thin (thin)	thank (thank)

them	then	tenth	that	path
think	thing	math	bathe	bath
these	thus	clothe	thud	this

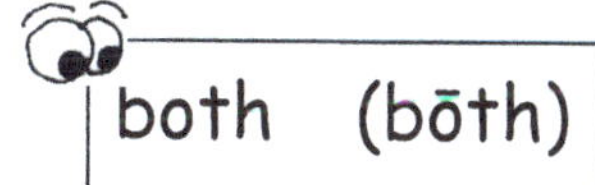

The Math Path

Beth says that math is a path to thinking. Beth makes the path to thinking nice. Both Bea and Sue think that Beth is nice.

The Paths

Kate asked, "Do you know if this is the path to my home, Bea?"

"I think so, Kate," Bea said. "This is the same path that I hike to camp. See, it is on the map."

"Oh, I see," Kate said. "The path to my home is the same as the path to the camp."

A Hot Day

The sun is hot today.
Hot, hot, hot.
The sun makes heat.
Hot, hot, heat.
The sun makes me
hot, hot, hot.
I am beat today.
Beat, beat, beat.

Towing Mike's Boat

Kate biked to the sea to see Mike.

Mike said, "Kate, I need my boat towed to the bay."

Kate said, "Dan made a neat boat and keeps it by the sea. Dan can tow a boat."

Dan sat making bait by the sea. Kate said, "Dan, meet Mike. Mike needs a boat towed to the bay."

"Nice to meet you, Mike. Kate, you can use my boat to tow Mike's boat. Can you pay me, Mike?"

Mike paid Dan and Kate towed Mike's boat to the bay.

F f

feet   fade   face   fame   foam   fake

gift   fee   fine   fast   fun   cuffs

fan   foot   soft   off   puff   safe

ph = (f)

photo (fō·tō)   phone (fōn)

Tim used his phone to take a photo. His phone can take a photo of my face. Tim's photo is fun to see.

Fay's Fine Fan

Fay had a faded fan. Fay said that it is fun to use a fan to feel cool, but she needed a fine fan, not a faded one. Fay phoned Sue to see if Sue had a fan for Fay to buy.

Sue said, "I make fine fans at home. You may come and buy a nice fan today."

_ch_   and   _tch

beach   cinch   chain   chin   chime   check
bunch   chop   chose   chat   cheap   chip

hatch   catch   itch   ditch   botch   notch
each   peach   inch   pinch   such   much

Chuck's Chimp

Chuck says, "I can teach my chimp to catch." Chuck pitches a peach to the chimp and says, "Catch."

It is a cinch for the chimp to catch the peach, but he does not pitch it back. He chomps on the peach.

Cheese Takes Time

Kate asked Ned, "Can you teach me to make cheese, Ned? I made some cheese today, and I botched it."

"You cannot make cheese in one day," said Ned. "It takes time to make cheese."

Chet and Nan

It is nice to see Chet and Nan at a chess match. Nan is a match for Chet at chess. It is fun to see them both play chess.

In a Pinch

My Mother and Father both think that math is fun and they teach it to me. They say, "It is a cinch to do math! In a pinch, you can ask us to aid you."

Fun Baths

Each day I take a fun bath. It is fun to bathe and take my boat into the bath. I have fun in my bath. My Mother does not need to make me bathe. I choose to bathe. I think it is fun.

sh

shop	shape	shake	sheet	she
shine	ship	shut	shed	shift

mush	cash	dash	dish	fish
gush	hush	ash	mash	shush

Beth Buys Fish

Beth buys fish at the fish shop by the bay. The fish shop has the best fish by the bay.

If Beth has the cash, she dashes to the fish shop to buy the fish. One time I ate fish at Beth's home.

Beth bakes fish dishes. She makes fish cakes. She mashes the fish and shapes the cakes on a dish. Beth makes fish cakes for me to buy, so that I can eat them at home.

5

L l

lace	lake	let	leaf	life	like
lock	load	lunch	lamp	last	land
sail	sale	mail	male	pale	pail
tail	tale	mill	hill	bell	fell
all	call	fall	hall	small	stall

Lill's Note to Bill

Bill,

I made up my shopping list. I may be at the mall all day today. Beth and I may eat lunch at the mall.

I think that all that I need to buy is on sale. I need to buy some lace. I hope that the lace is on sale. If the lace is not on sale, I may need some cash. Beth and I may be late.

~Lill

oatmeal   baseball   myself   into
seashell   sunshine   someplace   upon

Nell's Seashells

Nell finds seashells at the beach and sells them in her shop. She called me to say that she may have a sale at the end of May. I may buy some of Nell's seashells.

I like to look at seashells. One time Nell spilt seashells on the sand. I knelt to help pick them up. I like the feel of shells. I like to think that all of the shells know tales of life in the sea.

I like the sea, too. I like to pick seashells up and look at them. One day I may sail on a ship to a land that has lots of seashells.

black   blue   blow   block   blank
clean   clock   cloth   clue   clay
flow   flash   flag   fly   float
plane   plain   plant   plus   place
slow   slant   slice   slim   slush

At the Lake

One day Dad took us to the lake to play. My pals and I had fun playing ball. It is fun to slide in the mud. I like to play ball at the lake.

The Blue Sled

Pete is still not up. He is still sleeping, but he and Clint, his pal on the block, have to be at the lake at one p.m. to play on the ice and sled on the hill.

Later, Pete may have a tale to tell of sliding on the hill on his slick sled in the sleet and snow. Pete likes his slick blue sled. He keeps a cloth in his coat to keep his sled clean. He keeps it nice. Pete and Clint have fun on the ice.

calf (kaf)   salt (sawlt)   talk (tawk)

held	meld	scald	shelf	elf	self
gulf	silk	milk	elk	bulk	malt
spilt	felt	help	kelp	gulp	chalk

Milk and Cheese

Al held his pet calf by his side on the hill and held salt for the cow to lick. He liked to talk to his calf.

Al said, "I like milk. Do you?" Then he said, "I like cheese too, but I do not think that you like cheese."   The calf did not like cheese.

The Elf and the Flea

Ben asks his mom to tell him the tale of the elf and the flea. She says, "Ben, I have told you that tale a lot of times, but okay." Then she tells Ben the tale.

"The elf had a flea. He told the flea, 'I can teach you to fly I can flick you into the sky.'

The flea said, 'Thank you,' and he fled."

molt   bolt   folks   knoll   troll   toll
stroll   bold   sold   cold   hold   told

molted   bolting   strolling   knolls   trolls

The Elf King's Pets

The old Elf King has a pet calf and a colt on a small hill. They like to play on the knoll.

One day a man chased the calf and colt to the lake. The Elf King did not like that the man chased his pets. He told the man, "Be nice to my pets, and I may be nice to you. Be mean to my pets, and I may be mean to you."

Then the Elf King took his pets back to the knoll, and the man left. His pets liked to be back home and to play on the knoll.

_le

able (ā·bul)   battle (bat·tul)   amble (am·bul)

little   battle   table   middle   peddle
pickle   apple   uncle   fiddle   nettle
ample   amble   tinkle   sample   cattle

My Uncle Bill

Uncle Bill has an ample middle and says that he is able to eat a lot. Today he ambled in eating an apple and then he ate an ample meal at my table. He ate lots of cheese, apples, rolls and pickles.

Then Uncle Bill ambled to the barn to feed my cattle. He played my fiddle to the cattle in the barn. He played my fiddle and danced a little until the middle of the day.

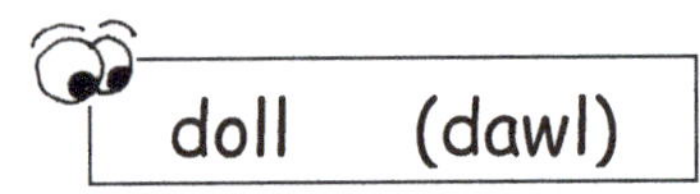

My Old Doll

My old doll sits alone all day long. Sometimes she looks like she is sleeping. She looks like a little child.

I like to hold my old doll.   I call my doll Bell. Some days she sits on the shelf all day, but I still play with Bell. I talk to my nice old doll, and she smiles back at me. I tell tales to my old doll until I fall asleep.

Blue Tail

Old folks sometimes tell old tall tales. Some tell the tale of a bold colt that had a blue tail. The tail looked like a blue plume. The old folks called the colt "Blue Tail."

Flies liked the colt's blue tail. The old folk called those flies "Blue Tail Flies."

6

R r

race   rain   raise   real   reach   ride
reed   rat   rate   rip   rich   ring
rest   red   rack   rope   rag   ramp
rock   road   rode   rice   ripe   rules

Rick's Red Rose

Rick ran a race in the rain
to get a real red rose for Fay.
He had to run up a ramp, reach
up and get a bell from a rack,
ring the bell and then run back.
He got the red rose and took it to Fay.

Then he said, "I'm going home to rest.
I hope that Fay likes the red rose. I
know that she likes roses."

rh_

Rhythm

Abe said, "I like to see Rose dance in her red hat. She has good rhythm."

"I have rhythm, too," Mike said.

Abe said, "Mike, a rhino has more rhythm than you do."

Mike smiled and said, "So? A rhino has more rhythm than you do, too."

Read and Red

read (rēd)   reads (rēdz)   red (red)   read (red)

I can read. Mom, read to me. Mom reads to me. Mom is reading to me. Mom read to me.

The Reading Rhyme
"Ray, read The Reading Rhyme."
Ray sat with his red book and read the rhyme.
"Red and read can rhyme, but bed and bead do not rhyme. As I lay on my bed, I read that red and read rhyme, but bead and read can rhyme, too."

R, are and _ar_ rhyme

chart   arm   barn   charm   card
spark   far   start   Carl   smart
harp   tar   march   harsh   dark

Carl's Car

"Carl, do you go by the marsh in your car?"

"I do, Ray. I go as far as the barn. It is far, but I may get to the barn by dark."

"Can you take me to the marsh?"

"I can, Ray. Get in the car. I will take you to the barn."

Mark's Harp

Carl's pal Mark plays the harp.

Mark said to Carl, "I cannot be in the marching band. I cannot march on the road and play the harp at the same time."

"I can help you, Mark," said Carl. "You can sit on a cart that I pull behind my car and play the harp. You and I can go behind the band. Then you can play the harp and be in the band at the same time."

"Thank you, Carl. You are a smart pal."

Air, _are, _air and _ear may rhyme

bare   pare   fare   rare   stare   share
fair   pair   stair   pear   bear   tear

A Rare Pair

If you care to go to the fair, the fare is fair. You can see a rare pair of colts at the fair. I like going to the fair to see the rare pair of colts there.

The Fair

"Is there a fair?" asked Art.
"The fair is in the park," said Ray.
"The park?" asked Art.
"It is there at the end of the road."
"Thank you, Ray. I can go to the fair there."

The Bears' Pears

Bears like to eat pears. They like to eat pears more than you think. They rub and shake pear trees to make the pears fall. Then they tear the pears with their teeth. The bears eat their pears under the pear trees.

Air, _ere and _eir may rhyme

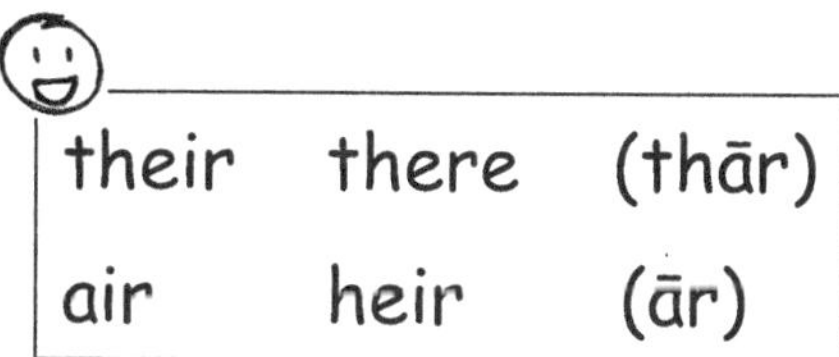

Their and There

There and their rhyme.
Here and heir do not rhyme
but heir and air do.
Their heir is not here,
he is there.

Heir is in **their**.
Do you see *heir* there?
Here is in **there**.
Do you see *here* there?

The Heir

Prince Carl is heir to the king's throne. His dad and mom told him that he is the prince, and Carl is their heir. One day Prince Carl is to be king. Then his son is to be the prince and Carl's heir, too.

Ear, _ear, _eer and _ere may rhyme

shear   near   tear   clear   dear
deer   cheer   peer   sheer   steer
mere   here   sphere

Dear Sir,

I had three birds at my home. One bird made a nest near here and nested there. One bird made its nest in an old tree at the church. My third bird made its nest in your deer barn. It is a smart and charming bird, but I fear it may be harmed if a cat or rat comes near its nest. May I come to your ranch and take my bird home to make its nest here?

Thank you,
Rose Marsh

Dear Rose,

Do come and take your bird home, but first you may eat at my home. You and I can share my iced tea. Do not fear, your bird shall not be harmed.

Ray Parks

Fur, _er_, _ir_, _ur_ and _ear_ may rhyme

fur	burn	curb	curl	church
her	fern	term	clerk	stern
stir	first	shirt	firm	third
earn	learn	earth	heard	search

Pearl's Bird

Pearl has a pert little bird. It is the first bird that she has had as a pet.

The bird perches on a fir tree and sings songs that can be heard in the church by the park.

The stern clerk says that Pearl's bird is full of mirth before it bursts into song, and it is like a blur when it flits from fir to birch. He says that the bird cannot come into the church, but he likes Pearl's bird.

The blue bird sat on her perch and sang a rare song.

An iceberg hit a ship, and the ship lurched and sank.

The men searched the earth for a herd of deer that ate ferns.

The sea stirred, churned and tossed the surf at the beach.

The clerk had dirt on his blue shirt.

Mom was filled with mirth on Earth Day.

The nurse's old purse burst at the seams as she sat on it.

You can learn as you earn.

Learning

Reading helps you to learn more. The sooner you learn to read, the better you learn. The more you learn, the more you may recall later.

Retell a Tale

Mike asked me to retell a tale that I had made up. I had to recall the tale and tell it once more. I had to redo it in my mind. It is not easy to retell a tale.

The Race

I cheered for my deer, but it ran in the rear. "It is clear," I said, "that my deer is not leading, but I can cheer him on until the end of the race."

The Seer

"Dear me," said the seer as he peered into his sphere. "This is going to be sad to hear. Your hair and beard must be sheared."

"You mean," said I, "I have to get my hair cut?

"I mean," said the seer, "You must be sheared."

The Elf's Deer

The elf said to the king, "There is a herd of deer near here. They play in the park and eat the pear trees."

The king said, "You can see the herd of deer there by the road. They may eat the pears, but I do not like them to eat the tree bark."

7

R r blends

br__ as in *brain*

brain   branch   brim   brand   broke
bride   braid   brick   brush   brunch

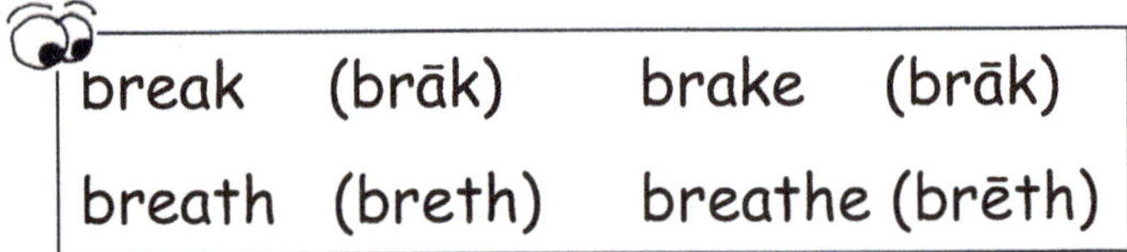

break   (brāk)   brake   (brāk)

breath (breth)   breathe (brēth)

Break the branch into thirds, and then bring the small branches to me.

Fill your brain to the brim and learn much more each day. Your brain cannot be too full.

Brenda

Brenda, my brother Bruce's bride, has nice black hair. She brushes and braids it once a day.

One day she broke her hair clip, and she said "I need a hair pin for my hair clip."

I had a hair pin. "Bring that hair clip to me," I said. She did.

I put a hair pin in it, and she said, "Do you have a pin for my broach? I broke that, too." I put a pin on her broach, and she said, "Thank you."

cr__ as in cream

cream   crow   creek   crust   craft

crash   crack   crane   crumb   crunched

creak   crate   crisp   crush   cross

Crab Meat

Craig likes to eat the meat of crabs and fish. He keeps crabs in a crock. He cooks the crab, cracks the crab shells and eats the crab meat. The crab meat is good to eat. Craig eats lots of crab meat.

The Crate of Bricks

Bruce told Brad, "Chet needs bricks to make a barn. Crank up the crane to lift this crate of bricks across the creek. Be careful not to break the crate. If the bricks fall and crash, they can crush things."

Brad did not break the crate. Chet got his bricks, and he made a good barn.

dr___ as in *drape*

drape   drip   drop   drag   dream   dry
drink   drill   dress   drab   drain   drum

The Creek Dream

I had a dream. I dreamed that I had nothing to drink, not one drop. I felt dry and drained. I beat a drum for rain, and the rain filled a creek. Then in my dream, I rode my bike to the creek and had a drink.

The Drab Dress

My sister needed a nice dress for a dance. She had a dress that looked drab, so she put lace on it. Then the dress was not drab. The drab dress looked like a dream. My sister will have fun in that nice dress.

 fr___ as in *frame*

frame   free   fry   frost   frosting
fresh   frail   frill   frog   fried
freed   froth   frank   freed   frogs

friend   (frend)

My Fish Friends

I helped my friend Fran catch fish. She had a lot of fish. She said to me, "Take two of the fish home."

I took two fish home and named them Fran and Frank. I put some food in their tank, but they did not like fruit, fried food or cream. They did not eat my food.

I said, "You must eat some food," but they did not eat.

I told my mother that the fish did not like my food.

My mother said, "They need be freed in the creek so that they can eat their food there."

I dropped Fran and Frank back in the creek. I hope that they ate something there.

tr__ as in *tree*

tree   try   trap   trade   train
treat   track   truck   tray   trick
trim   trail   trace   trip   trust

The Troll Tracker

Carl is a tracker. Once he tracked trolls across a creek. The trolls did not like being tracked, so they used tricks to hide their trail. They crossed the creek from time to time and hid their trash in the earth. Carl tried to track them to their home, but in the end he lost the trail.

On the Farm

Frank likes his farm a lot. He rises at the break of day, hears frogs croaking and sees cranes flying in the sky. On the farm Frank makes cream cheese from milk and cream in an old crock.

Frank likes his days at the farm. He says that each day is crammed with life.

pr__ as in *pride*

pride	praise	proof	prop	press
prank	price	print	prod	preach
prompt	pry	prune	prime	prom

The Prince's Pride

The Prince liked his friends a lot, but they called him a fool. One day they planned to play a prank on him.

His friends knew that the prince did not read, but put his books on a shelf to look as if he did. They asked a printer to print a blank book. Then they told the prince of a book that they had read and liked.

"I'll buy it," said the Prince. He did, but before he put it on the shelf, he looked at it and knew that he had a blank book.

His friends told a princess to ask the Prince if he had read his book.

The Prince said to her, "My friends said that they had read it, but it is not much to read. It is a blank book that tells the tale of those that are not true friends. They tried to make a fool of me, but I am going to learn to read." The Prince's friends lost his trust.

8

R r blends

scr__ as in *scrap*

scrap   scratch   script   screech   scrunch
screen   scrimp   scrub   scrape   scream

The King's Scroll

The King sat on his throne and read a scroll. He read that Prince Carl had eaten all of a troll's rolls and had not paid for them. The troll had made his rolls from scratch. He had to sell scrap for his funds. The troll had screeched and screamed that the King must make Prince Carl pay him.

Reading the scroll upset the King. He told the Prince to pay the troll more than three times the price of the rolls. The Prince paid a lot for those rolls that he ate.

Lill's Script

Lill made a script for a film. She scrubbed homes to get the funds to take her script to the coast. She scrimped and scraped to get her script to the screen.

In the end Lill made her script, and that began her life of making scripts.

     © First Stage Publishing Company

shr_ as in *shrimp*

shriek (shrēk)

shrimp   shrill   shrug   shredding
shred   shrub   shrunk   shrinking

The Crow

Fran heard the shrill call of a crow from a small shrub. That crow shrieked so hard that Fran's ears hurt. Crows make shrill calls to their mates.

Shredding Paper

Dan asked, "Did you shred paper all day?"

Mike shrugged and said, "No, the sun is still up. The day has not ended. There is still a lot of paper left to shred."

Shrimp

Beth likes to eat seafood. She eats shrimp and crabmeat, but shrinks from eating sea slugs. Beth has eaten shrimp most of her life. She is eating shrimp now. Do you like to eat shrimp?

spr__ as in *spree*

spree   spray   sprite   spruce   sprain
spring   spry   sprung   sprinkle   sprint

The Elf King and Spring

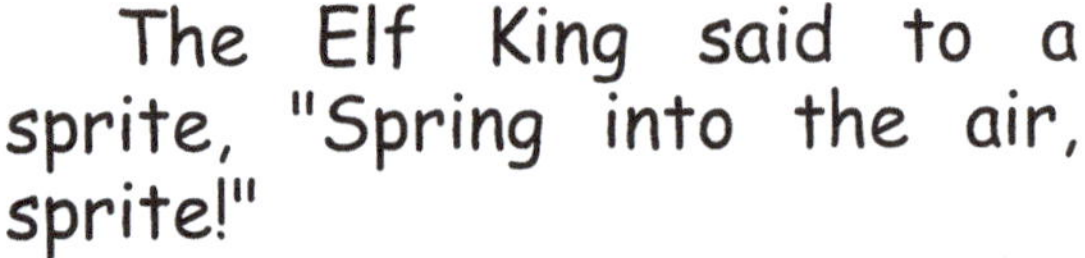

The Elf King said to a sprite, "Spring into the air, sprite!"

The sprite sprang into the air, but she did not stay up.

The Elf King said, "Sprite, do it once more, but this time climb up that spruce tree, then leap."

The sprite said, "I can leap into the spray in the sea, but I cannot leap from a tree. If I do, I may sprain my leg. I am a spry sprite, but I do not need to fall to know that it is safer to leap into the sea. I look before I leap."

The Elf King said, "Try sprinting before you spring."

The sprite sprinted. She leaped up and sailed into the air. Her face lit up. She smiled.

The Elf King smiled too as he said, "Since you sprang so nicely, I shall call you Spring."

str__ as in *street*

street string strap stripe strand stream
strip   stress strict strike strain stretch

Streak

My sister Ann is a strong runner. She is so fast that she is called Streak. She stretches before she runs, so she has no strain or stress. She runs on the street to the beach and along the beach to the dock.

Each day Ann tries to beat the time she set for the day before. She says, "To run the best that you can, each day you must do your best."

Rose Plays Ball

Rose plays baseball. One day she struck the ball so hard that it sailed across the park. Rose says, "No strain, no gain."

Rose plays for fun and for her team. I cheer for Rose and her team.

thr_ as in *three*

three throw throat thrust
thrill throb throne thrift thrall

The King's Scrap

The King stood up from his throne and told his friends a tale of his scrap with three mean men. The three men had made fun of the King and Prince Carl. They had hurt the King's son and made him cry.

The mean men told the king, "You are too old to make us stop." They did not know that he is a spry old king, as bold and as strong as three men.

The King stopped the men by saying, "Is it good to tease a boy and make him cry? No, it is not!"

Today those men are nice. The King's tale thrilled his friends.

9

R r and O

_**or**_ as in *cord*

cord	for	corn	horn	form
or	horse	north	force	forth
nor	cork	sort	short	sport

My Birthday

It stormed the morning of my birth. My father had to force his horse to cross a stream to get to Mother's doctor.

The doctor lived far from the farm. My mother sat there on the old porch, hoping to hear my father coming home.

As my father came close to home, he started blowing his horn. Mother says that she heard the horn. Father and the doctor came in time for my birthday.

_ore as in more

more   ore   score   sore   store
core   shore   snore   tore   bore

The Old Men

There are a lot of old men at noontime each day at the store by the shore of the lake. They tell tales of the old days. In those days, the men used gold ore to pay their bills.

Today there is not much ore left in the hills. The old men recall their old chores of digging ore from the earth. It is nice to hear those old men tell of dreams that they once had back then, in the old days.

oar as in *board*

board   soar   soared   roar   roars
boar   oar   boarded   hoard   hoards

☀ The men used oars to row the boat.

☀ Can you hear the roar of the sea?

☀ If you hoard food, it may go bad.

☀ The planes soared to the sky.

The Boar on the Boat

A boat that had three men and an old boar on board pulled out to sea. The men said that they had fresh boar meat to take to their ship, but the boar had other things in mind.

The boar roared, smashed the boat and tossed the men into the sea. Then the boar made it back to the shore. From then on, the men said one thing about old boars: old boars are not boring.

our as in *your*

your　four　pour　court　source　fourth
yours　poured　pouring　courts　sources

☀ Four men played songs at the King's court.

☀ At the beach I found an endless source of sand for your garden.

☀ The fourth ball court is on your left.

True Riches

"Can you help me to find true riches?" Kate asked a seer.

The seer said, "To find riches you need to set your course for the source of all true riches. That source is in your heart.

Your heart is the source of all true riches. To be rich you must feel rich. Then, the good in your heart pours forth more riches than four men at a king's court, and your heart soars."

83

_oor as in *poor*

poor   boor   moor   door floor

A Moored Boat

A poor man moored his boat at a dock.

"That is my dock," said a boor. "Untie your boat. You cannot tie it here at my dock."

The poor man untied his boat, and sailed to a dock on the other side of the lake to moor his boat there. He said, "I think it may be fun to moor my boat on the other side, but not by that old boor."

The Door in the Floor

Pam once had a home with a door in the floor.

"A door in the floor?" you may ask.

It is true, a door in the floor. The floor had a door that led to a room beneath the floor. To get to the room you had to use that door in the floor.

Ann's Scar

Ann had a scar on the skin of her leg.

"Your scar looks bad," said Kate. "Did you fall?"

"I was skating and I slipped," said Ann. "A skater coming by hurt my leg. Skating along on the ice is fun, but it can be a risk. One must be careful of other skaters."

Playing in the Snow

Spence once had a red sled and a pair of skates. He had fun playing with his sled in the snow. Folks called him "Spark" in those days.

They said, "Spark can skate like they do on TV. His red sled can slide so fast that his scarf flies off of his neck."

He did fly like a flying spark. He sure had fun.

Today Spence sees Ann take her sled to the hill and thinks of the days that he did the same. He liked racing his sled on the hill, and she likes racing hers there, too.

A Star?

Beth's old steer stood in its stall stamping the earth. Steam rose from the old steer's nose. The steer stared at a stack of corn stalks.

Beth said, "Stand still. Stay there. I can put some corn stalks in your stall for you to eat. Then I must feed the rest of the stock."

Beth did all of her chores and started up the stairs to her home. She looked up at something in the sky that made her stop in her tracks.

It shined like a star, but did not stay in one place. It seemed to start, skim across the sky, stop for her to see it, and then leave.

Beth said, "Did I see a falling star or a flying disk?"

She stared at the sky for some time, but she did not see another thing that started and stopped as it made its trip across the sky.

Slim's Slacks

Slim slid on the snow on a hill. He slipped, fell and tore his slacks.

Slim's mother said, "Go slow, Slim."

"I am going slow, Mom," said Slim. "I slide and spin going fast or slow."

Smoky and the Snail

Our dog Smoky is barking a lot. My dad says that he must be barking at a skunk.

He looks at Smoky, then he says, "Smoky, you are nuts. That is not a thing to bark at. It is a snail."

Smoky sniffs at the snail. He smells it for a bit, then he tries to scare it. He runs close, barks and snarls at the snail, but it does not care.

Smoky rolls the snail on its back and tastes it. Smoky does not like the taste. A snail is not the best tasting food for a dog's snack. He pushes the slick snail and slides it into the bushes. Then Smoky tires and falls asleep.

Mike's Fine Scarf

Mike had a nice scarf, but it shrank in the rain.

"May I buy that scarf for my son?" Lill asked Mike. "He's small. I think that he may like it. The scarf would look great on him."

"Lill, you cannot pay me for this scarf, but you may take it as a gift for your son."

"That is nice of you, Mike. Thank you so much."

10

J j

Jack　Jill　job　jade　jet　jeep
joke　just　junk　juice　jolt　jiggle
jam　jug　jail　jump　jot　June

A Jet Joke

Jack and Jill hiked to the store to fetch some jam and juice.

Jack heard a jet plane, and the noise jolted him. He jumped and Jill said, "Do you just jump when a jet flies by, or do you jump when flies jet by, too?"

The Jade Stones

Jane had some jade stones. She said, "See them shine, Jill. I like them. They shine a lot."

"Did you buy them?" asked Jill.

"I traded some old junk for them, and then I shined them. Jack may jump for joy when he sees them."

"I can just see him, Jane. Jack may jump a lot. He likes stones that shine."

G g (j) as in *gem* (jem)

giant	gentle	cage	stage	change
huge	range	hinge	fringe	edge
judge	bridge	dodge	badge	pledge

Ginger the Giant

In the old days, there lived a gentle giant named Ginger. He lived in a lodge on the ridge near the fringe of a huge hedge.

Ginger said that it cost too much for a gentle giant to ride on a coach, but it is cheap for an elf to ride. So to ride on the coach, the giant used magic to change into an elf.

Not His Day

Jim trudged up the hill to see an old bridge at the edge of Dodge Ridge. A big rock rolled by and almost hit him. He had to roll in the dirt to dodge it. He got dirt on his shirt and had to trudge back to the lodge to change.

"Grant," Jim said to the man that ran the lodge, "this has not been my day."

The Golden Goat

An old man heard a strange tale of a goat made golden by magic.

He said, "If I find it, I can be rich in my old age."

So he left home and trudged here and there in search of the golden goat.

One day a stranger told him, "The goat is near here. You can see it, but do not touch it. The folks here do not like strangers to see or feel their golden goat."

The old man saw the golden goat standing behind an old gate, near a hedge.

"Gosh," he said as he gaped at the goat. Then he felt the goat's coat. The goat lunged at the gate and knocked the gate down.

Someone banged a huge gong, and the old man heard someone shout, "Get him!" The old man gasped and ran to a boat on the beach.

On the boat the old man said, "The old golden goat is nice to look at, but a golden goat is just an old goat that is made of gold. I cannot get it. I cannot sell it. I do not need that old golden goat."

gl_ as in *glass*

glass   glide   gleam   glow   glue   gloss
glare   gloom   glance   glob   glee   globe

The Glowing Globe

Glen and Jill passed by a store that had a globe in a glass case. The globe glowed in the dark. The globe gleamed and glinted there as they made a trip to the store to get it.

Then Jill looked at the globe and said, "Glen, that globe is made of cheap glass and there is a glob of glue on it. Not all that glows in the dark is good."

The glow faded and Glen did not buy the globe.

Eggshell Art

Glenda, the girl in the blue dress, uses glue and eggshells to make art. She glues the shells on glass to make them gleam and glow in the sun. They are grand. It is good to see them shine.

gn_ as in *gnat* (nat)

gnat   gnu   gnarl   gnome   gnashed

The Gnome's Hat

The gnome sat by a gnarled tree full of gnats. Some gnats sat on the gnome's hat and upset the gnome so much that he gnashed his teeth. The gnome knocked the gnats off of his hat and the gnats left.

The Gnu

On the African plains, gnus may be safe, but only if the big cats do not chase them. You can bet that the gnus do not like  to be eaten. So if the big cats show signs that they need to eat, the gnus just run off as fast as they can.

gr__ as in *grab*

grab grade great grill grand grow
gruff graph grass grid grate grin

A Great Graph

George got an A grade for making a good graph. He felt grand.

His gruff old grandpa grinned and said, "My grandson did a good job. He made a great graph. He is not letting the grass grow under his feet."

A Lack of Rain

Grace grows grain and grapes on her farm. She is grim. There is no rain, and the grain is only half grown. She cleans the grime from her hands and reaches out to grip a spade to turn the earth.

"I grow good crops," she says, "but sometimes the lack of rain gets to me. The grain and grapes do not grow if there is no rain."

gu_ (g) as in *guess* (ges)

guest   guess   guard   guilt   gull   guy

guide   gulch   gulp   gust   guff   gulf

guitar (gi·tar)

Gus and Gene

Gus and Gene's guests all liked to hear music. So Gus and Gene guided them to a room that had a guitar and bells in it. Gus played the guitar and sang some songs, and Gene rang the bells. Their guests clapped along to the songs.

Gus said, "I guess that our guests liked those songs."

Seagulls

Jean and Jill sat by the seaside and looked at the seagulls flying by. Jill chewed gum and tossed it into the sea. A seagull ate the gum.

"Oh, no!" Jill said, feeling some guilt. "That seagull is going to have gum in its gut. I guess I cannot toss gum on the beach. I need to think before I do something like that."

"Good thinking," Jean said.

Acting

Jack acted in a stage play. His sage old coach said, "You have been cheated. You lost all of your gems. That man cheated you. Show your rage."

Jack did a good job. He read the script and played the part.

Popcorn Days

On cold days at home, the frost clung to the bark of the trees. The smoke from the chimney rose into the dark sky. Mom made popcorn. Mom called us to come in and the kids filled up eating popcorn. The kids strung popcorn to hang on the trees for the birds and also made popcorn balls to eat later. Popcorn balls tasted the best on cold days.

Sitting by the roaring fire in the fireplace, Mom melted butter to coat the popcorn. It tasted so good. Making popcorn is fun.

The Red Rock Stage

Two bad men named Pack Rat Bob and Jake the Snake had been holding up the stagecoach to Red Rock for four months. Someone had to put a stop to their crimes.

Big Duke said, "I can ride the stage to Red Rock and stop Pack Rat and Snake in their tracks."

Pack Rat and Snake stopped Big Duke's stage two miles from Red Rock.

"This is a holdup," said Pack Rat. "Give us the cash box."

"Not today," said Big Duke. "Stop in your tracks."

Big Duke had the drop on Pack Rat and Snake. That ended the holdups.

V v

vain   vane   van   vice   vote   vale
vase   vest   vet   verse   vine   verb

cave   shave   save   gave   cove   grove
stove   clove   hive   dive   eve   drove

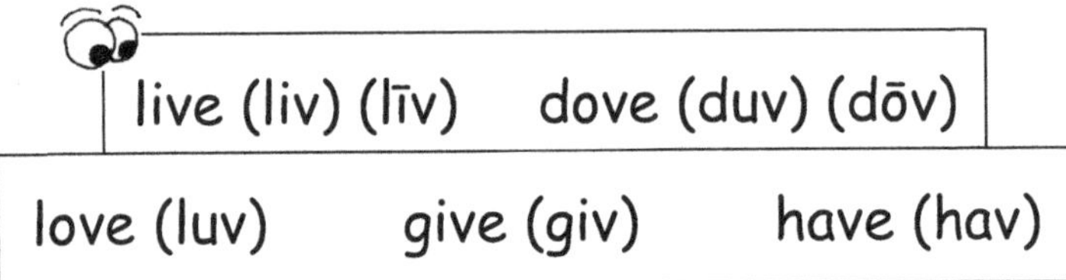

live (liv) (līv)   dove (duv) (dōv)

love (luv)   give (giv)   have (hav)

My Dove

I love my life. I live with a live dove. My dove flies near me as I dive into the sea.

I dove into the sea one day, and my dove dove by me, but not into the sea. My dove dove into the sky.

My Vet's Van

My vet has a van that he can live in. His van has a stove and a vent to let out the smoke. He camps out in his van. One time he drove it to see a cave by a cove near the beach. He loves his van.

Use Your Vote

"Vote for me," said the vain man as he hooked his thumbs in his vest and pushed out his chest.

"Give me your vote. I can give you the best deal."

My mother said, "I voted for you last time, but you did not give us much more than the hole in the donut. You have asked for my vote in vain. I cannot give my vote to you. You have to earn my vote."

One or More of a Kind

leaf   leaves   In the fall the leaves turn golden.

knife   knives   Knives are to be used with care.

half   halves   My pal cut an apple into two halves.

life   lives   Some say, "Cats have nine lives."

scarf   scarves   Beth had many lovely scarves.

calf   calves   Al has new calves on his farm.

shelf   shelves   Jane's shelves are full of books.

loaf   loaves   I om baked two loaves of bread.

W w

with   wake   west   wade   wire   waste
wait   wipe   will   weak   wise   waist
week   ware   wish   wage   world   worked
wasp   wand   want   wash   watch   wanted

was (wuz)   walk (wawk)   were (wur)

Walt's Wet Wig

Walt wore a woven wig in the rain. Was that wise? The rain soaked Walt's wig. Walt wished that he had not worn it. He wept by the wall, wiped his wet eyes and waited for the rain to stop. Then he walked on his way.

In Winter

In the winter, Ann likes to skate on the ice, slide on the hill in the snow, and make snowmen. She loves cold days with lots of frost.

Ann wakes each day and waits for the snow. She wants the snow to fall so that she can play in it.

wh_ (hw) and wh_ (h)

what   when   where   which   why
white   wheel   while   wheat   whim
whirl   whisk   whale   whine   whip

whose (hooz)   whole (hōl)   whom (hoom)

Wool

After Will shears the white sheep, Wilma will spin the wool on the spinning wheel. When the wool is spun, Wilma will weave the white wool into cloth.

When will Wilma weave the cloth?
Why did Will shear the sheep?
Who will spin the wool?
Where do we find wool?

White Tires

"My car has white tires. I got them at the Whale Wire Wheel shop."
"You did? What did you pay for them?"
"A whole lot, but they are nice."
"From whom did you buy them?"
"From a nice man named Walt Whale."

wr__ (r)

write   wrist   wreath   wrong   wring
wrote   wreck   wrench   wretch   wretched

Writing to Will

Will had Walt's wrench, but Will had not paid for it. Walt wrote a note to Will. He wrote, "When will you write me a check for my wrench, Will? Write me back when you can and let me know."

Will wrote back, "I will pay you when I have tested the wrench. It may be the wrong kind."

Jane's Note

Jane wrinkled her forehead and began to write a note to Jake.

Her note said, "Jake, I heard that you hurt your wrist while you were wrestling. That must have been wretched. Did your team wrap up the game with a win? I hope you won.

Love, Jane"

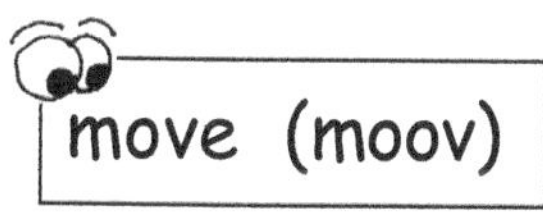

Moving to a New Home

Mike and Jan moved to a new home. Someone told Mike and Jan that ghosts were living there.

Jan was afraid of moving there, but Mike said, "I'll prove to you that they are wrong about the ghosts. You have nothing to fear."

That was not as smooth a task as Mike had hoped. In fact, it was hard to put Jan's fears to rest. The house had five ghosts.

At first the ghosts loved that Jan and Mike moved in, but Jan and Mike were too loud and they wrecked the ghosts' peace. The ghosts did not like having Jan and Mike living with them. The ghosts began to writhe and wring their hands and wail all day long.

Soon Jan and Mike said, "We will let the ghosts have their home back." Jan and Mike moved away to a good home with no ghosts living in it.

Writing and Reading

Ruth says that writing and reading are two things that she likes to do. She uses e-mail to write notes to pen pals in far-off lands, and they write back to her.

Wilma, one of Ruth's pen pals, lives on a ranch. She has a pet colt and a wren that sits on her wrist. She wrote to Ruth to tell her of the day that her colt was born. She calls her colt Roamer because he likes to roam on the ranch. She wrote one day to invite Ruth to come to the ranch and ride Roamer.

Jean, another pen pal, likes her life at the sea. She has a red boat that she rows to the beach to buy things. She has seen many lands. Her mother and father are teaching her to read and write on the boat.

Sometimes the pen pals wrap up gifts with wrapping paper and strong tape, and send them to each other. Ruth is pleased that she can read and write. Ruth's pen pals have added a lot to her life.

tw__

twice twig twinge twine twist
tweet twill tweed twitch twirl
tweak twin twelve twang twitter

Twelve Birds

Walt saw twelve birds twitch and twitter on a twig. The birds twisted and twirled small twigs like twine. They were making nests. "Tweet, tweet!" they twittered.

Twins

"Twins see eye to eye," Sue said.

"What does that mean?" asked Walt.

Sue said, "It may mean that one twin is as tall as the other. Also, it may mean that one twin knows what the other is thinking."

Walt said, "I guess some sayings have more than one meaning."

SW_

sweet swam sweep swirl swell
swamp swiftly swing swipe sway
swim swore swarm switch swap

The Swan's Swamp

We watched a swan fly over and land in a swamp. The swan was swift in the swamp.

The swan swam swiftly, swished its tail and swept the swamp. The water swirled. A swarm of flies rose out of the swamp. It was a sweet sight to the swan. That swan liked to eat flies.

_aw_ as in *law* (law) | all (awl)

saw   flaw   hawk   fawn   straw   claw
jaw   thaw   draw   crawl   flaw   paw

My Day

One day I saw a fawn on the lawn eating a rose. Then I looked at a crow cawing in a tree and saw a hawk fly by. I had a fine time watching the fawn and the birds that day.

_ew as in *new* (noo) and *few* (fyoo)

chew   blew   grew   drew   threw   new
knew   crew   dew   brew   newt
hew   hewn   pew   skew   skewer   fewer

Chewing Gum

The whole crew on my ship chewed gum. A few stuck the gum under a bench to hide it from my view, but some threw it on the deck.

When I stepped on the gum, it stuck to my shoe. Then I knew that the crew was chewing gum.

ow as in *low* (lō) and *cow* (kow)

low	show	grow	blow	know	throw
owe	flown	bowl	bow	shown	growth

cow	how	owl	growl	howl	brown
plow	vow	brow	bow	wow	crowd

A Row Boat

Mike said, "I know how to row a boat."

"Wow!" Bill said as he slapped his brow. "Rowing a boat in the lake is hard to do. Can you teach me how to row the boat? "

The Cow Knows

The brown cow had to tow a sled in the snow.

"How now, brown cow?" asked the owl.

The cow said, "You know, go slow." The cow towed the sled and plowed the snow.

The owl said, "Now, that's good. Towing a sled on the ice is easy, but towing a sled in the snow is slow. Go, cow, go!"

12

U u

unit	unite	unites	unicorn	utensils	unify
up	under	uncle	unseen	untied	upper
us	utter	ugly	unload	update	umpire

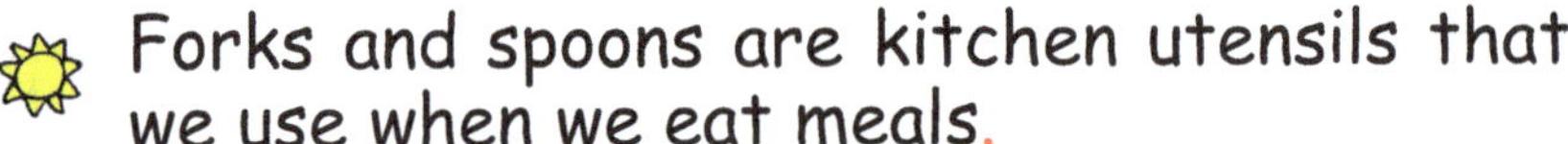 Forks and spoons are kitchen utensils that we use when we eat meals.

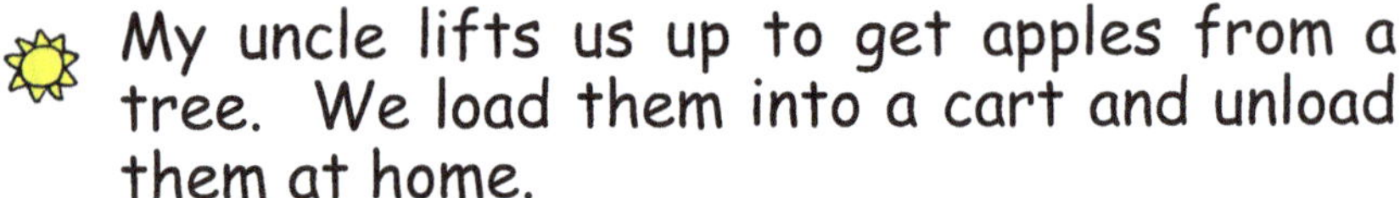 My uncle lifts us up to get apples from a tree. We load them into a cart and unload them at home.

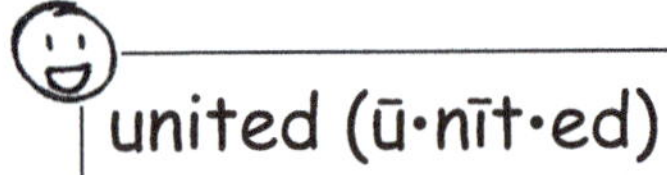 Umpires use rules to judge baseball games.

united (ū·nīt·ed)

The United States

The United States are states that are united. The American flag is red, white and blue.

Each state is a unit. We can see state borders on maps, but borders on land cannot be seen.

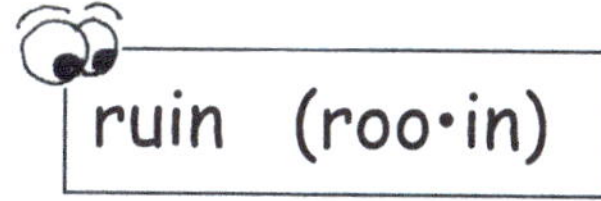

_ui_ as in *suit* (soot)

suit   bruise   juice   cruise   fruit

u_e as in *rude* (rood)

rude   flute   fluke   dude   crude   brute

_u_e as in *fuse* (fyooz)

fuse   use   cute   mule   cure

A Crude Brute

A crude brute broke the rules by playing a flute while the duke slept. The Queen said, "Stop it, dude. That's rude. The duke does not like to hear flutes when he is sleeping."

June's Mule

June's cute mule liked to chew on an old boot. One day the mule knocked over a fruit juice can and ruined June's suit while it chewed her boot.

June said, "You are a crude dude, Mule. It is rude to use my old boot to chew on, and my suit is ruined, but T still think you're cute."

_au_ as in *cause* (kawz)

sauce	haunt	launch	jaunt	taunt
fraud	Paul	maul	gauze	ault
pause	taut	haul	clause	fault

Paul's Boat

Paul had to haul his old boat to the lake to launch it. He needed help.

His crew grew because his pals knew that he needed help to haul the boat to the lake. His crew hooked a rope to the boat and pulled it taut. Then they hauled the boat all the way to the lake and Paul launched his boat.

Saul's Saw

Saul paused while he was sawing wood. He had been sawing wood out on the lawn since dawn.

Then June called, "Lunch time! Saul, I've made lunch with a cake and a fine fruit sauce." Saul stopped, put his saw down, and went in to eat his lunch with his wife.

_aught as in *caught* (kawt)

caught   taught   daughter   fraught

Aunt Maude

Aunt Maude has lived on a farm her whole life. She was taught to milk a cow when she was a little girl. She worked hard. She filled a lot of milk pails.

Once Aunt Maude stood in front of the barn and watched as a red hawk circled in the air, then dove down and caught a mouse in the straw. Hawks like to eat mice.

Aunt Maude's barn had a lot of mice. When Aunt Maude's daughter Paula grew up, Aunt Maude taught her how to catch the mice in the barn.

Paula was hard working like her mother. One day she went to her mother and said, "There is not one mouse in the barn now. I think that I have caught the last one."

Qu_ qu_ (kw)

quit   quake   queen   quack   quote
quill   quick   quite   quiet   quilt

square   squat   squint   squirm   squab
squawk   squirt   squeal   squeak   squid

The Queen's Trip

The queen walked to the town square to buy some gifts. When she was there, she heard "quack."

"It must be a duck," she said. Then she heard a squeak.

"That's quite odd. Ducks don't squeak, and mice don't quack."

She came around the corner and there were two ducks and two mice. She jumped and dropped the gifts that she had bought. The mice ran to the corner and the ducks quacked and waddled away, too. The ducks and mice were not good friends for the Queen, and she was glad to see them leave.

cannot	=	can't	is not	= isn't
do not	=	don't	it is	= it's
were not	=	weren't	I am	= I'm
will not	=	won't	he is	= he's
I will	=	I'll	we will	= we'll

A Chance Meeting

By chance, two old pals met one day at a coffee shop. One of them said, "I can't believe it. Aren't you the Queen's son, Carl?"

"Yes, I'm the Prince. Do I know you?"

"I'm Lee Sharp. We went to the same school. Won't you have lunch with my wife and me? I know she'd love to meet you. She's a fan of yours."

"Oh, really? I'm sorry, I'm on my way to see the Queen, so I can't have lunch with you now. Oh, dear me. It's noon, and I have to go. It was nice to see you. Bye."

"Who's that?" asked Lee's wife.

Lee said, "It was a pal of mine, Prince Carl. We went to the same school."

"Don't tell me that you know the Prince and you didn't ask me to meet him!"

"I asked him to have lunch with us, but he had to dash off to meet the Queen. He's a nice chap, but sadly he didn't have time for lunch."

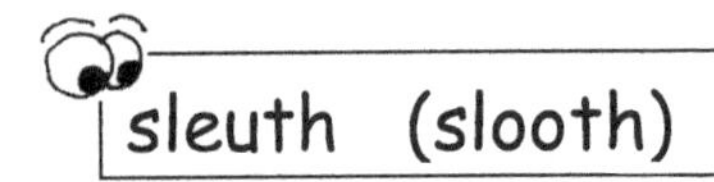

Duke the Sleuth

Duke the Sleuth was waiting for a note from Big Bruce. Luke, a rude dude, knocked on the door and walked into the room.

"I have news," he said. He took out a note and threw it on Duke's square desk. "Read it. You have the clue about the boots that you have been looking for."

Duke said, "Tell your boss thanks. Don't slam the door on your way out."

Luke fumed as he left. Duke read the note, which said, "A goat was seen with June's mule. They were both chewing on your old boots."

Duke said, "It's a good thing that I have new boots. My good old boots are like chewing gum now. I hope that those two like them quite as much as I did."

The Haunted House

Wrapped in our shawls, we went for a jaunt to an old haunted house. The house was very dark and quiet, but we heard a creaking door. We weren't daunted by the ghost tales that Father told us because Mother said that she had never seen a ghost. She told the truth. We did not see even one ghost at the haunted house.

13

O o

I i

E e

O o

_oo_ as in *book* (buuk)

look	stood	good	wood	shook
cook	nook	took	hook	brook

My Book

I was in a good mood, so I took some food and my new book to read down by the cool brook in the woods. The book was about a brood of chicks on a farm. It was a good book to read by the brook.

_oo_ as in *food* (food)

room	root	goose	bloom	boost
brood	moon	mood	tooth	roost
moose	coop	boom	boon	soon

A Good Mood

I saw a chick roost in its coop. Then a goose flew by. There was a moose in the woods and the flowers were in bloom. I was in a good mood when the moon came up.

_ou_ as in *could* (kuud)

would   could   should

Be Kind

Meg said, "Pam, it would be good if we could always be kind to others. Would you help me to greet shoppers at the store? I would be so thankful if you could help me."

"What would I have to do?" asked Pam.

"All you would have to do is smile and say 'Good Day!' We should try to get the shoppers to say it, too. If we all said 'Good Day!' at the same time, those words could be heard around the world."

_ou_ as in *noun* (nown)

our   round   about   sour   sound   proud
bout   cloud   ground   count   bound   found

A Good Ship

Did you hear the story about the ship they found grounded on a sandbank? It was pounded by huge waves for around twenty-four hours, but it's still sound. That ship is a good ship.

_ough has more than one sound

Rhymes With

Doe rhymes with though and dough.
Puff rhymes with tough, rough and enough.
Off rhymes with cough and trough.
Not rhymes with thought, bought, and brought.
Too rhymes with through.

Though it may seem tough to remember that off and cough rhyme, give it enough thought, and it won't be too rough.

Words with _ough

- Bread is made of dough.

- Though we all tugged very hard, the tough rope never broke.

- Sandpaper is quite rough.

- The pigs ate at a trough. One pig had a cough.

- I brought my money and I thought about what I bought.

- The sun is shining through the clouds.

_oy_ as in *boy*

joy   coy   toy   Roy   ploy   Joyce

_oi_ as in *voice*

choice boil   spoil   point   toil   join
coil   soil   joint   noise   oil   coin

Mother's Choices

Roy and Troy's mother said, "You boys have a choice about how I cook our meat today. Should I fry the meat in oil, broil it in the oven or boil it in water?"

The boys were playing with their toys and making a lot of noise. They didn't hear their mother's voice.

She raised her voice and said, "Roy and Troy, should I fry, broil or boil the meat?" They still didn't hear her. She shouted, "Do you want to eat today?"

They heard that and paused. Roy asked Troy, "Do we want to eat today?" They both nodded their heads up and down and said, "Yes, mother."

Their mother said, "Oh, the joys of having boys!" She flipped a coin to make her choice.

I i

_igh as in *high* (hī)

high   sigh   thigh   right   tight   night
light   bright   might   slight   fright   sight

Stars at Night

You might see bright lights in the sky on a dark night. The stars are such a nice bright sight in a dark sky.

A Good Knight's Work

One dark night a knight stopped his horse at the sight of a child who was afraid of a sharp and wicked thorn bush. The knight cut the bush off at its roots and said to the bush, "May blight wither your roots so that no one else will take fright at your thorns."

The child sighed, "Sir Knight, you have done a good night's work."

The knight was proud because he thought that the child had said that he was a good knight.

_ie as in *pie* (pī)

pie   tie   die   lie   vie   skies   cried

The Pie

Meg and her friend Fran played a game to win a pie. Both tried hard to win the game, but it was a tie. They flipped a coin. The judge cried, "Meg, you won! Get your pie."

Meg said, "Fran, both of us can eat the pie. It is huge."

_ie_ as in *field* (fēld)

field   shriek   siege   piece   chief   priest

Talking about Peace

In a field where the birds twittered and shrieked in the trees, the chiefs of two groups met to talk about peace. They shared pieces of bread with each other and sang a song. They talked and joked together and called each other, "Friend."

E e

_ei_ as in *eight* (āt)

veil   skein   vein   beige   eight

The Queen's Veil

The beige veil on the queen's head weighed more than eight coins and was adorned with red thread. The queen felt proud in her beige veil, but her neighbors said that it was too bad that the Queen's nice face could not be seen when she wore her veil.

_ei_ as in *weird* (wērd)

weird   ceiling   neither   either   priest

Fun Time

It's not weird to have a good time when all of your friends are at work. It's all right. Take some time to have fun. Your friends will want to have fun too when they are not working.

My friend Jean says, "You have a choice. Either work or have fun." Jean likes having fun. I have more fun when my work is done.

> # I Before E
>
> Write **i** before **e**, except after **c**
> as in ceiling, receive and receipt,
> or like ī as in height,
> or when sounded like ā
> as in neighbor and weigh,
> or like ē as in weird, either, and
> neither.

My Neighbor Marcus

My neighbor Marcus likes to rest and take it easy. He always takes the chance to either sit down on his chair or sleep on his sofa.

If you gave him a choice between giving up his chair or his sofa, he would say, Neither!

I like to rest on both. My chair holds my weight, and my sofa fits my height."

_ea_ as in *bead* (bēd)

breathe eat weave lead bead read
wheat leaf leave neat plead real

The Beanstalk

Jack pleaded with Bea to read the tale of the beanstalk. The beanstalk had big leaves and thick vines that reached to the sky. Bea took a seat and read the story to Jack. Sometimes she stopped to catch her breath. Jack liked when Bea read to him.

_ea_ as in and *head* (hed)

head lead thread dread read breath

Leaves

Some leaves that are green in the spring turn red in the fall. They fall from the trees in the winter when they are dead. Other leaves stay green all year round.

More Than a Hill

I led my hiking team up a high hill. My feet felt like they were made of lead. When I reached the top, I said, "I'm so tired!"

My teammate said, "Today I read that the old hill is more than a hill. It's over a thousand feet high."

The Land of Real Reindeer

In the far north is a land called Lapland where real reindeer live, work and play. There, the Lapps raise great herds of reindeer. The deer are called reindeer because they are guided with reins just like horses.

The Lapps use lap robes to keep warm because Lapland has a lot of snow, and it is cold. They use the reindeer to pull their sleighs and haul their freight.

Y y

year   yes   yet   yell   yard   yam
yarn   yield   youth   yawn   yoke   yolk
you   your   you're yours   you'll you'd

__y like (ī) in *sky* (skī)

try   by   dye   eye   style   rhyme

Troy's Hair

Troy dyed his hair the color of an egg yolk.

"You're in style, Troy," his Dad said, "but soon you'll have to try to buy a different hair color. That color just doesn't suit you."

__ey like (ā) in *they* (thā)

hey   prey   whey   they   obey   grey

Yam Pies

Young Dan's mother said that she needed egg yolks to make yam pies. The youth yawned and went to the backyard.

"Why are you looking there?" his mother asked. "The eggs are in the barn. You'll go all the way to the barn if you want your yam pie."

_y as in *baby* (bā·bē)

baby   lady   happy   sunny   daily   shady

The Gifts

One year my mother and father told my sister and me, "You'll find lovely gifts in the backyard."

Our gifts wagged their tails and yelped. They were two baby puppies named Lady and Happy.

I still see them now the way they were then, young and happy. Lady would dance and Happy would bark along when we played music. Lady and Happy were our best gifts when we were young.

Sometimes I yearn for those days of our youth. They were good sunny days when we played with our puppies and chased them around the yard.

_y_ as in *myth* (mith)

myth   hymn   rhythm   mystery

Hymn

Our singer tells us tales by singing hymns. We sway with the rhythm while the singer sings about old myths. The rhythm of a hymn can make a myth seem real once more.

The Eye in the Sky

Yesterday I read a myth about the sun called The Eye in the Sky. The style of the story was new to me. A myth does not always tell true facts, but it tells us how someone thought about things or events once upon a time, a long time ago.

The girl in the story calls the sun "the eye in the sky." She says that the sun watches over us and gives us light all day long.

Z z

zoo   zip   zone   zoom   zero   zigzag

doze   maze   crazy   haze   quiz   snooze

gaze   graze   glaze   blaze   whiz   freeze

buzz   jazz   froze   size   ooze   sneeze

The Zebra in the Zoo

The zebra stood quietly in the zoo and stretched to reach the highest leaves on a tree. As it grazed, the zebra looked up and gazed at birds as they made a zigzag path across the sky. Then the zebra zipped away.

The Whiz Kid

On a farmer's field there was a maze that no one could get through. Liz said that she could do it. She took her dog Zero with her and left bits of bite-sized dog treats at the entrance and along the way as she walked through the maze.

When Liz got to the center of the maze, she let Zero go free. He found his way back to all of his treats and she walked behind him. When she came out, people shouted, "Liz is a whiz!"

X x (ks) as in *box* (boks)

ax   coax   next   tax   wax   mix

fix   ox   flex   hoax   flax   fax

fox   six   text   lax   flux   duplex

The Boxed Fox

Once there was a fox that made its way into a waxed box filled with a mix of six great snacks.

He ate so much that he got stuck in the box and was in a real fix.

Then a mouse came by, ate the box and freed the fox. Some foxes eat mice, but not this fox. The mouse saved the fox's life. Sometimes help comes from strange places.

one fox   two foxes   one box   two boxes

Sam fixed boxes.   I fixed two axes.

Liz mixes waxes.   The girl mixed the flax.

Broken Boxes

Sam's friend Tex dropped his ax on Sam's boxes and broke six of them. When Sam saw his broken boxes, he said, "If a box is broken and has not been fixed, no one will be able to use it. Please, fix broken things and you won't need to buy them again."

X like (z) in *xylophone*
(zī•lo•fōn)

The Xylophone

A little boy named Xavier found a real xylophone and put it in his toy box to play with. Xavier made pretty sounds with his xylophone. He could sing songs with the tunes that he played. His friends liked to listen to him and to sing along when he played music on his xylophone.

Two or More Syllables

The first vowel is long in words like

music   tiger   lady   dining   hotel   pilot
baker   later   baby   hoping   flavor super

Choices

Dan was asked, "What do you think would be fun to do when you get older? Would you prefer to be a pilot who flies super jets or a baker who bakes cakes with new flavors? How about a person who plays music? Would you like to work in a hotel?"

Dan said, "If I were a pilot, that would be super, but baking cakes could be fun, too. I guess I could do both or even something else."

Hotels

Hotels are more than places to sleep. Some have music, nice dining rooms and some even have bakers who bake bread with great flavors.

The first vowel is short in words like

number (num·bur)   picture (pik·chur)
splendid   structure
princess   trumpet
shelter   hundred

Dinner

The writer took his wife to a diner to eat dinner in the evening. The flavors of the meal that they ate were super. Later, the writer and his wife saw a lady baking bread in a bakery. They bought some bread for their baby to eat for dinner.

The Trip

A princess took a trip that was one hundred miles long. She saw a number of splendid structures. There were sky scrapers and shelters and tunnels. The most splendid structure was a lovely bridge. She took pictures of all of the things that she saw.

When a Quarter Was Worth More

My grandfather told me that when he was young, a quarter was worth more than it is now. It went farther at the store and was harder to earn. He remembers that he worked for an hour cleaning up after a party for the first quarter he ever made. He heard his father murmur to his mother that he had a lot of spirit and deserved to be paid a quarter for his work.

Grandpa had a hard time choosing what to buy with that quarter. For example, he could have bought a lot of marbles or even a quart of syrup, but he decided to buy a little statue of a cherub for his mother's garden. Times were different then. A quarter was worth a lot of money.

The Puzzle

The little boys struggled to put the purple pieces of their puzzle in the right places to make a picture of an apple.

Their uncle was tickled by their struggle. He had a twinkle in his eye. He said, "I've never seen a purple apple before."

Ducks and Rain

When it rains too much, it floods the brook. The rain soon makes pools for the ducks in the woods. Ducks look forward to a good rain. Rain puts them in a good mood.

Paul's Flute

When Paul played his flute, he chewed on the end, and the flute cracked. Paul knew that the crack he made grew too big to be fixed. His flute was ruined.

The few people that heard about his broken flute were sad because they knew that he could not take his flute with him when they all went on a cruise. He would need a new flute to play for the folks on the cruise. They all got together and raised money to buy Paul a new flute.

Jobs

The sailor was an actor who later became a director.

My counselor was my mentor.

Go to school to learn to be a reader, a writer, a speller and a leader.

Mother said, "It would be helpful if you filled up a cupful of water for the plants, and take a cupful for yourself, too."

We saw two lovely and graceful swans swimming on the lake.

My puppy is lovable but capable of biting.

You are a remarkable human being.

Just because something is portable doesn't mean that it's easy to carry.

My dad says that I am a playful armful. My mom says that I am an armful of energy. Both say that they are doubtful that I will ever stop being a willful child.

When your shoe is untied, please tie the shoe strings. If you are unable to do so, your shoe will be unsafe for walking. You could trip on an untied shoelace.

Jack and Spike

One day three-year-old Jack met a big dog named Spike on the hill. Spike liked Jack and licked his face. Then Jack started to cry for help.

Jill ran up the hill and said, "Don't cry, Jack. Spike doesn't bite."

Jack cried, "I know he doesn't bite, but I think he was tasting me. If he likes me, he'll eat me. If he doesn't like me, then he might bite me."

The Three Wishes

Once there was a woman who found a magic lamp. She knew what to do with it. She rubbed it and out popped a genie who said, "You can have three wishes, but take care what you wish for." That was a threat. "Take your time," he grinned.

The woman sat down and said, "I must think, think, think." She sat there all day long. She had read about genies and their tricks. She knew that a genie could make her very unhappy if she made poor wishes. When she was ready, she called the genie.

The genie smiled a wicked smile and said, "Take care what you wish for. Ask, and it shall be yours. Speak!"

The woman said, "My first wish is this. I wish that no wish of mine shall bring hurt or harm to anyone. Second, I wish for enough wealth for my family, friends and myself to be happy. Third, I wish for us all to enjoy our lives in good health."

The genie's smile faded as he said, "Granted." Then he asked, "How did you get to be so smart?"

The woman beamed and said, "I read and I think before I speak."

The Dictionary

You have learned to read, and now you will be able to read dictionaries to learn about words that you do not know.

Dictionary spellings show readers how to spell words, and they also show you how to pronounce them. For example, the sound spellings of *there*, *their* and *there* are all pronounced the same (**thair**), and dictionaries show that.

Dictionaries provide the meanings of words. Some dictionaries also teach you which language the words came from.

Many types of dictionaries may be found online, in a library or a bookstore. If you do not understand a word, look it up in a dictionary to learn how to pronounce the word and what the word means.

Dear Reader,

Welcome to the world of reading. Words are all around you in books, newspapers, magazines, on signs, and on the internet. You can travel through time and space in an instant and learn about health, history, and how to make things.   You can read about people and countries that existed long ago.

You will be able to use the library and can read about fantasy and magic, share the feelings of real and imaginary characters in stories and find out how to protect the earth. It's all there for you to read and you have the skills to do so.

Now you will be able to read and communicate with people from all over the world instantly with e-mail and find information on almost any subject with the internet.

The key to this wonderful world is reading. Now you have the key.

Congratulations!
Ruth and Thomas Velasquez

CPSIA information can be obtained at www.ICGtesting.com
Printed in the USA
BVOW11s1435180315

392144BV00003B/4/P